T0365627

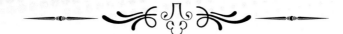

Breaking Down the Wall of
SILENCE

Carlos A. Rivera

Layout Designer: Ranilo Cabo

To order additional copies of this book, contact:
Xlibris
844-714-8691
www.Xlibris.com
Orders@Xlibris.com

ISBN: Softcover   978-1-4363-0992-9
            Hardcover   978-1-4363-0993-6
            EBook   978-1-6698-3794-7

Library of Congress Control Number: 2007909841

Print information available on the last page

Rev. date: 07/13/2022

BREAKING DOWN THE WALL OF
SILENCE

by Carlos A. Rivera

For the majestic artistry that lives within all.

–Carlos A. Rivera

In loving memory of our son, Carlos A. Rivera. It was his wish to have this book published, and now his wish has finally come true.

We love you and missed you very much, son.

Your spirit lives on forever.

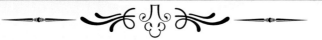

CONTENTS

Foreword

It has been said that writing can be the soul's salvation. Indeed there exists no outlet more liberating than that provided by the mere act of putting pen to paper.

Yet nowhere is the soul more in need of liberating than in the springtime of life adolescence. This transitional phase takes our young people with countless demands. Demands for a purpose, for an identity, for a call to arms against the sins of generations past, and for so much more.

The writer, Carlos Rivera, whose experiences you are about to share, lays bare his soul as he grapples with those demands. As you commence your foray into his words you will quickly detect a maturity beyond what is normally expected of a person his age. More pages turned will only confirm your instincts. Indeed, Carlos has gulped from the bittersweet cup of experience where most have only sipped.

"Poetry," wrote Matthew Arnold, "is nothing less than the perfect speech of man, that in which he comes nearest to be able to utter the truth".

Rivera's truth is hardly uttered, but is more akin to having been shouted over a loudspeaker, such us the way of breaking down the wall of silence.

Here is to the tumble.

—John Corazzar

Acknowledgments

First and foremost, I would like to thank my lord and savior Jesus Christ for being my guide, my light, my refuge, and my protector; my parents, brothers, family, and friends for their constant support and inspiration; and John Corazzar for kindly writing the foreword. Thanks to Ana Maria Mastrogiacomo for allowing me to take advantage of her amazing talent and include "Unfamiliar Touch" as part of Breaking Down the Wall Of Silence, and to Jacqueline Wright for contributing to this project. Last but not least, I thank Mary Joe Hoffman for inspiring the class to write and for taking the challenge to teach a group of high school students. This class certainly helped me open my eyes to discover a part of myself and the peers I had never seen before. Thank you all for being part of my life and for allowing me to be part of yours.

Intro

Survival of the Fittest

Darkness pours through the valley like a great flood washing away the incandescent
sunlight helplessly caught at the wake of dusk.
A veil of shadows hides the torments of this land and it sets over's the horizon.

The charcoal clouds soar through the turbulent raven sky with pride and wisdom. Lighting recurrently
strikes down the earth with barbaric authority announcing the dawn of hell.

Simultaneously all existing matter trembles at the command of nature and
the thunder echoes beyond human sight.

Carelessly, the bitter blows of wind sweep away the dead leaves of the
trees into the mystic darkness beneath them.

Starving carnivorous vulture descend from the sky at the scent of rotten flesh.
Ripping apart flesh from bone they crowd and devour their prey.
This is the call of war, the survival of the fittest.

The weak shall fall and the strong survive
There are no rules, no limitations, no boundaries, no alliances, no nothing.
It is pure loneliness and despair, cruelty and corruption, darkness and murder.
This is the wakeup call at which every living creature embraces the
battle without question or doubt.

I

I come from the land of sugarcane and sunburning days
I am the seed of my nation
The "Mariachi" that sings "Rancheras"
Rhythm, salsa, cumbia, mambo
It is my adventurous heart that travels day and night
from coast to coast
I sing for love and laughter
It is an inspiration that never dies
I am made of chocolate honey
From Spaniard and Mayan backbone
Proud of my semifortunate past
I am willing to stride for days to come
I am proud to be Latino
And represent the Spanish guitar
Playing the notes of my journey in life

Fallen Star

Shine bright, gentle star
You are I in the sky
Shine bright day and night
Twisting fast out of sight
Fast pace, brutal fall
Out of bounce in a split
Heat harlot in the mud
Now trapped can't get out
Fight, fight, don't give up
Turn left, right, and back
Drowning fast, gentle star
Fight, fight, don't give up

Endlessly Waiting to Rise Once Again

I wait
Day after day
With misery and pain
For I have fallen
For I can't find a way to rise once again

I wait for challenge
I wait for my palace
I wait for the burning sun to rise
And shine its light over me
For the wondering birds to sing that song of dynasty
For the Indian hunter to cry at last
For the animals to mate and rise
For misery to end and die
For a spell to be cast
I wait for the dawn of the day
I wait to see on everlasting day

I wait for the bats to fly away
And for the fish to swim safe

I wait for the stars to shine
I wait for the only one
I wait for the moon to set
I wait
I cry
I hope
I whisper
I pray to finally see an everlasting face
And for my lord to help me once again

I wait with courage
I wait with strength
I wait with faith
I wait day after day

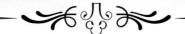

This Is
Goodbye

You told me you had other plans
Little did I know it was with another man
You asked for money 'cause you were short on cash
Without me knowing you spent it on his ass
You said it was girls' night out
When in fact you stayed home and fucked him all night
Now I know why the long hours
Going-away weekends
and nights out.

I wanna hear no more lies
No more cries
You're a fucking bitch
Get out of my sight

Did you actually think you could play this game for long?
I ain't no slave
I ain't no fool

Please don't pretend you're hurt by your act
You're phony and full of crap
I just can't believe I let you stay in my house
But now it's over and you are the one that looses at last
'cause I got my house, money, health, dignity, and honor

All I want is for you to leave and don't look back
Take your shirts and your skirts
'cause that's all you got
Keep walking forward don't look back
You're a piece of trash
I almost feel sorry for your ass

I wanna hear no more lies
No more cries
This is goodbye

Broken Heart

Miles away

Within my sphere

Lies my broken heart

Shattered in tears

Desert Sand

With heart set on Sky

I lay on burning salty

desert sand

Until you entered my life

Crystal Clear

Far deep inside a sea of darkness
I exist in a box of crystal and crafters
Water is cold like arctic
My freedom taken away
My wings can't extend
It is infinite space

My eyes wide open yet blinded by nothing
I carry the burden of hatred
I long to escape this solitude
I long to be free and fly
Fly over the seven seas
I'll let the light be my guidance
I'll let the winds take place
I will know the difference between dark and light
I will enjoy the bliss of laughter
But until then let hope live on for eternity
For I don't know when my freedom will come along
I have no more tears to shed
No more strength to fight
For deep inside is a sea of darkness

HUSH

For deep inside my inner side
I hear a voice that tells me to hush
But I won't listen
I refuse to hold these words and bite my tongue
I will break down the wall of silence that holds me back
For if I don't speak out my mind and heart
I'll forever be trapped in the past

I hate the fact that she played me
I hate the fact that we can't ever be friends
But truthfully I rather forget who she was
'Cause now that she's gone
I have everything but bitching stuck in my mind

Nothing was ever good enough
Everything had to be done her way or no way at all
She was a control freak
Daddy's girl, fake in his eyes
She played the victim role all the time
As if she had no intentions to hurt those revolving
in her malignant trap

The hurting has ceased, now my healing and loudness begins

The Beach

Went to the beach yesterday

Met a girl there

She touched my abs under the sun

Near a palm tree she sat

Soon a bag lady came by

Selling cheap jewels she was

Bought one necklace from her

The hot girl looked at me asking, "Where is mine?"

"Too bad," I said, "I only got money for mine".

A slap in the face I got

Thought it was funny so I laughed

Hit me again and walked away

"That's OK I didn't care . . .

. . . next please"

Nasty Girl

You are such a flirt
You lead me on
Told me things
That made me fall
Now I know you're just a flirt
That simply looks for a screw

You move on from guy to guy
Like a trashy dog lost in the park
You suck more dicks like nobody else I know
To me you're toilet paper filled with shit and
nothing better than a slut

You ain't got nothing to offer
But simply your dirty sexual organ
That has been around the block
more than once

You're nasty
You're trashy
You're nasty girl

Naked

I arrived home at 1:00 p.m. this afternoon. I can't completely recall what it is that went on last night, but surely it was a night I wish could be forgotten. It was utterly foolish to think that "E" would make the night move pleasant and fun—how stupid or drunk was I? To think that I always swore that I would never fall into the trap of drugs and alcohol.

The previous night was wild. I refer to it as a "Sexual Revolution." Slowly and helplessly I was caught in the act of sex and rebellion. I became unrestrained and lost control for solely one wild, erotic, and rebellious night. The excitements of these new uncanny desires and pleasures captured my mind, heart, soul, and body. I became uncontrollably addicted to wild fun at the expense of "E."

My boys and I went to the underground last night. Drugs, alcohol, and women were the main attractions of the night. We left the party at approximately 1:15 a.m. (give or take). But we were not alone, four girls, probably in the age range of 19–22 accompanied us to the ABC motel on Dougall.

Instantly sexual acts erupted like an atomic bomb released without warning. It was a simple pleasurable fuck . . . without meaning . . . without commitment. I can't recall the actual act; I can just remember taking heavy doses of "E" and alcohol.

I woke up this morning at around 11:00 a.m. to find myself surrounded by a completely trashed room and buddies lying on the dirty floor. I was shocked to learn those bitches had left with little recollection of the events that took place last night. I jumped off the bed and searched for my clothes that were nowhere to be found. I was left naked, without clothes and money, but most importantly without my dignity and morality. Simply covered with a blanket, I sat on the edge of the bed looking out the window blaming nobody but myself. I stripped myself from self-respect and decency and paid the price for such brutality. I was left naked and disgusted by my actions. I was left . . . NAKED!

Gold and Diamonds

Gold and diamonds are not enough

Life itself is not enough

If I had to pick the world's

greatest treasure . . .

. . . I would pick you

This Moment

This moment I wanna take some time to tell you how much I care
To tell you that no matter what happens I'll always
be there by your side
When the sky is dark and you can't see the light I'll be there

This moment is the moment I've been waiting for
The moment you and I embrace as one
Through thick and thin we'll make it together
We will grow old with the moon and the stars

I love the glow in your face
And your smile makes everything OK
I love the curls of your hair and the passion you give away
I love the mystery in your eyes and the compassion in your heart
I just can't wait to have you in my arms

How Do I Tell Thee?

How to I tell thee?
That your love has given me a new vision
That thou and I are meant to be
That there is no other place I rather be

How do I tell thee?
That every time thou looks deep inside my brown eyes
I see our picture-perfect future
Without hesitation I lose myself within
your magnificence
That even if nothing is said I know thou is thee
And thou loves me

How do I tell thee?
That I dare not fear
That I offer thou the moon and the stars
That I thank thee, daring, for shinning in
my life now so bright
That I trust to go blind and let you guide
me through raven path

How do I tell thee?
That day by day I need your presence
That every night and day I pray to earn your love

That I consider thou my water and bread
Without thee I am lost, thou, please follow
me to run blooming days ahead
I'll forever be grateful for that heavenly day

How do I tell thee?
That I can no longer go on
That every hive needs its queen
That every queen needs a king
That thou has stolen my heart
That my love is that gift
That thou love is my key

How do I tell thee?
That if heaven permits I'll make you my queen
That I will never allow thou to shed
a lonely tear
That never will I doubt our pact
That I will forever respect, honor, and love thee

How do I tell thee?
How do I tell thee
That sun shine bright blooming stars
I loved you then and I love you now

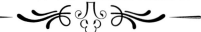

Addiction

An anomalous artery I have adopted since that day an
electric-driven discharge arrested my heart
It is like never-ending stairs reaching the sky
It is a feeling of passion, eroticism,
and addiction I cannot deny

Skin to skin, I can feel your passionate familiar touch
That has me floating in space and drowning
in an ocean of lust

I am helplessly addicted to the way you look
deep inside my brown eyes
Without strength I surrender to the touch that
leaves me naked in the dark

I am addicted to your full red lips that feel like wet
cream over my body on those erotic nights.

Your long shimmering spring-scented brunette hair that
covers you breasts when you stand naked in my eyes.
Your bronze skin hardly pressed against me
I am addicted to the feeling of your breasts in my hands
And the way our tongues wrap like hardcore chocolate
candy that never loosens

Its sweetening flavor during our act of sexual
expression every night
I'm addicted to your Oscar de la Renta
perfume aroma
It drives me wild
It turns me on
I'm addicted to the way you unbutton
my shirt and take off my pants
And the way I return the favor without
question or doubt in my mind
We become animals of nature and surrender
to this expression

This is addiction
It feels like jumping off a cliff, like frying
without wings in the sky,
Like losing control of a roller coaster that crushes,
breaking through the ground, and penetrating until it
reaches the melting magma deep inside
It is a delicious moment that captivates my mind and
surrenders my body to the act.

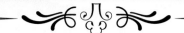

Archangel

He is the guardian
The guardian of time past and yet to come
For eternity he was chosen to fight

For thousands of years a story was passed
A legend that foretold the coming of the chosen one
The one that would take lives and rest them intact until the was nearby

He passed away and was brought back to life by the powerful being beyond the sky
In the shadows and light he exists
On the face of the earth he walks
On the mystical waters he doesn't understand he rejoices

In the sky we've conquered he lives
For eternity he is the guardian
That has taken my love from my side and put her to sleep until revelations
The last chapter starts

This is his gift
This is his curse
This is my loss

UnboundedWounds

I watched seven sails, sail seven directions
It was my heart twisted in affection
I touched the moon and the stars
That night you and I made love under the heavenly sky
You, my love, gave me all I have
I'll forever be grateful for every moment we spent together in this life

I saw the sky turn pitch-black
And a rose that died
I saw a bird fly in the dark
It was my heart wandering in cries
I saw the sun make love to the sea
As I saw the rest of my life disappear

As I traveled to infinity and back
I found the answers to all the questions I had
So many times have I seen the setting of the sun
Without a doubt you're still in my heart

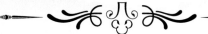

Heaven Café

All day I've been waiting for tonight
for it's the only time you are mine and I am yours
for it's the only time we reunite

As the sky begins to darken
my mind starts to wonder

The crescent moon has defeated the light
the shadows and fog have taken over the night
my eyes slowly drift into space
for my heart is searching the dream I chase

In this dream there is no pain
no anger
no hate

It's only you and I embracing as one
but as the sky begins to brighten
I find my way back to where I had started

And as the day goes on
I long to be asleep
For in my dreams you are mine and I am yours
For in my dreams we are back together as we once before

If at any time during the sun's rule I seem lost
And my eyes drift into space
Please turn off the lights
For I rather be lost in the warmth of darkness
And find my way to heaven café

And so the moon and the stars are my witness
That every night I dream of you
That every night I hope to be with you
And no matter how hard it is
I will find you
'cause the shadows of darkness are upon me
As they were once with you

The Things I Fear

When I met you
I was scared of you

Now that I know you
I'm scared of liking you

Now that I like you
I'm afraid of loving you

Now that I love you
I'm afraid of losing you

Until the End

So much depends upon our will
Our will to strive in life
Our will to embrace and fight

So much depends upon our hope
Hope to win at the end of the battle
Hope to overcome all shadows

So much depends upon our faith
To dance with angels in the sky
To reach the moon and the stars

May God look upon me with grace and glory
So I can proclaim victory at the end of my story

Unfamiliar Touch

The touch of you burns my hand like snow

It's a piercing feeling my body doesn't want to know

So long in darkness it hates the light

But for some reason it decides not to fight

My heart shall surrender because of your touch

Yet you must remember it will only swell so much

As soon as you let go I'll be back in solitude

In a place where no one sees and the light is often rude

It's a world you cannot enter and no one ever will

Simple and exquisite my entire world lies still

The only time there is sunshine is when I see your face

I see rainbows only when I'm locked in your embrace

The beauty only lasts so long and soon the storms roll in

It's a game that always teases me-impossible to win.

The Thought of Escaping My Prison

The thought to escape and be free has taken over my mind

The thought to be recognized once again as is

To liberate my soul trapped inside

To become one with nature and dust

So strong this repulsion is

So painful my life is

Let me go and be free

Like the birds in the sky can be

Like the waves in the ocean

I wanna be strong and be lost in emotion

Strong like the king of the jungle

Humble at the feet of dysfunction

If it wasn't for thee walls that keep me in

I'll be out and free

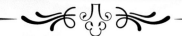

I Close My Eyes and Imagine

I close my eyes and imagine a white gate that opens the frontier to a divine world. Its tiled golden streets
lead through a silver city full of love, happiness, prosperity, and peace.
At night its full yellowish moon brings light to darkness and rest to its inhabitants. Crickets sing in a passive
harmonized rhythm. A gentle breeze blows through the glasslands and the stars sparkle up in the heavens.
The smile brings the beautiful musical notes of the robin throughout the land,
and the dear down to the stream.

The rough and aggressive sapphire waters clash with the crystal made rocks that sit at shore. The clouds
gently and slowly navigate the cheerful baby blue sky.

I close my eyes and imagine . . .

Victory
(Glorious to See the Light)

How glorious it is to see the light

Shining on my face

Never-ending ardor and tranquility inside

Lost in darkness

Now I shine

I proclaim VICTORY!

My Reflection

Shady no more

The mirror is clear bronze

There is no more mud on the walls

Spirit wondering mind

Birds fly high above the clouds

Feral tiger venomous ready to fight

Snake willing to bite

Confessions

To you, oh glorious God, I confess I was not the sweetest
peach in the basket,
but rather rotten from time to time.
To you I confess my ups and downs
To you, oh Jesus Christ, I confess what I really
feel like deep inside
Without fear of confinement or rejection I confess
my inner-reflection

Oh, dear Lord, I have committed so many sins
Sins that I can no longer take back, but ask to forgive
I saw my house tumble and blame spread
I still hold record toward those I love and cherish

I confess to have allowed myself to be driven
be earthy obscene delights
Delights you commanded should not be given a try

I have taken a bite out of the rotten apple of sin
Now I ask you to take me back and guide me
out of this raven sphere
I confess to you to you, oh Lord, without detail for you
know my heart and soul
I confess
I ask for forgiveness

ENOUGH

ENOUGH!
THESE FEELINGS I CAN NO LONGER DENY I WILL
FOREVER KEEP THEM CLOSE TO MY HEART

ENOUGH!
I NEED TO CHANGE MY LIFE
GIVE IT A TURN FOR A BETTER TOMORROW AND HOPE
ONE DAY REACH THE SKY

ENOUGH!
I CAN NO LONGER KEEP TRYING TO FIGHT
WITHOUT GUIDANCE IN MY LIFE

ENOUGH!
I HAVE STUMBLED SO MANY TIMES
NOW LET ME STOP ENDLESSLY WAITING TO RISE OVER AGAIN
AND CONFESS MY SINS TO FLY HIGH AMONG THE STARS
TO REACH MY HEAVENLY LORD THAT SITS
HIGH ABOVE THE CLOUDS

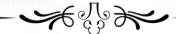

Salvador

I was bad, I was wrong

I was mild, I was cold

I turn you down, you took me in

The wings around me kept me warm

The narrow path guide me through

The voice I heard made me believe

You as a whole set me free

You as a whole gave me peace

I stop and cherish the minute you came to me

I stop and cherish the moment I found you within me

From Autumn to Spring

A frigid leaf once fell off a tree
Spiraling any wisk way like a fallen star
From high above the celestial sky

It voyaged through dead valleys and glaciers across the land

For soil and water it searched
But found itself trapped in earthy delights

One day the almost extinguish leaf
Prayed to Jesus Christ
Who gave this fallen leaf all strength to fight?

From dead soils it traveled
Until one day it landed in glaciers
And flourished with blooming faith and courage

Now an everlasting green stands tall and strong in the valley of death
Shining bright to escape the darkness within every
corner of its existing time

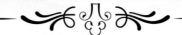

Survivor

I stumbled on stones lying on the valley of death
Fell and drowned in crimson tears of tribulations and distress

Sword to sword
Tooth for a tooth
Eye for an eye

I have survived
I am a survivor

I am a love maker
Not a heartbreaker
A symbol of peace
Not war

A gladiator I have become
Dominating the dark
And consumed by light
I am a survivor

Thank You

Thank you, dear Jesus,
For your everlasting love, symbolically marked on
the day you were crucified
I give you the praise
You have shown me the lights

I am grateful for my blessings
I am grateful for my struggles
I realize no one can love like you do
I realize you are the way
The narrow path that is hard to follow but bless at
the end of all battles

Thank you, Lord,
I will no longer look back or hold another cry
I will never allow a wall of silence to built between you and I

Thank you, Lord,
For my marvelous family
And misfortune past that molded me into the person I am
Thank you, Jesus,
You are my water and bread

Thank you
For my divine right to live

I pray and raise my hand for whose lives are marked with
abandonment, exportation, famine, affection, homelessness·
Oh dear Jesus! I cannot list them all
It is painful and it hurts me immensely
I ask you to let your sacred blood rain over every soul

Thank you, Father
Amen

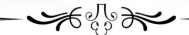

The One Thing I Know for Sure

The one thing I know for sure is that when I get up in the morning
That as I get ready to face the world, he's still with me.
Through hatred and darkness he will guide me
From pain and loneliness he will save me

From the shadows of the crowd he will pull me away
To give me his kingdom of grace
Without him, I might as well be dead

The one thing I know for sure is that god loves me unconditionally
'cause his love is infinite
His love is forgiving
His love does not keep track of wrong
It is not self-seeking

This is the one thing I know for sure

You and I

You and I
We don't seem to change, do we?
Everything around us ages as if there was no
Tomorrow

But when I look at you, I can only see the smile
I saw the day I first met you.
Luminous and enchanting our lives are turning
And maybe sometimes it seems as if we are
Growing apart, when we're really not

Life may bring
Sadness and perils,
One cannot stand alone
It will bring you
Challenges and anxiety
It will bring you
Happiness and accomplishment
It will keep our friendship and help us grow
We are friends on this EARTH
Where GOD has put us together to help us
Through it all,
And in heaven I will see you smiling
Like I have before.

(Amazing Grace)

Amazing Grace, how sweet the sound,
That saved a wretch like me . . .
I once was lost but now am found,
Was blind, but now, I see.

'Twas Grace that taught . . .
My heart to fear.
And Grace, my fears relieved.
How precious did that Grace appear? . . .
The hour I first believed.

Through many dangles, toils and snares . . .
We have already come.
'Twas Grace that brought us safe thus far . . .
And Grace will lead us home.

The Lord has promised good to me . . .
His word my hope secures.
He will my shield and portion be . . .
As long as life endures.

When we've been here a thousand years . . .
Bright shining as the sun.
We've no less days to sing God's praise . . .
Then when we've first begun.

Amazing Grace, how sweet the sound,
That saved a wretch like me . . .
I once was lost but now am found,
Was blind, but now, I see.

It's a Beautiful Day

When I opened up my eyes today
Felt the sun shining on my face
Got up and looked up the sky
To see the light that shines from above
Unmasked my window and sensed the breeze
gingerly streaming through my hair
Without restriction
Without obstruction
Without fear of reprisal
Felt the sand of peace
Tasted the whisper of the careless winds
Felt the smell of nature that was heavenly made
As I closed my eyes and thanked God for such a beautiful day
I also asked him to answer all my prayers

I woke up and realized that everything is going my way
Through my prayers I have seen the world through heaven's eyes
And now I see the beautiful things that you never think about
It's amazing how we don't appreciate our blessings
Nor do we take time to give grace to our heavenly Lord that
helps us create pure destinies

I was lost in maze with doubts and regrets
Now I look forward with focus and zest
I am living, I am thankful
I am breathing, I am grateful

Today is the day that I can say without procrastination
That I'm willing to put the past behind me in
company of redemption
No more regrets, loneliness, or darkness
I can't afford to shed another tear
For I got rid of all pain and fears
For God has given me strength and will

At last I have ascended to the top of the pyramid
I was sent to raise
For he gave me strength and power
Dignity, humility, and courage to overcome all
shame and darkness
I have no more to detain my inner self
The doors that have opened will never close again
I am living in this world
I wanna make a change
I won't give up; I'll fight to the end

The walls have tumbled and enclosure ceased
There is no limit to what I can render or dream
'cause my day has set length come to be
And there is nobody that can take that away from me
But the mighty God, Jesus Christ
Who lives on forever in nature and I

Can You Hear What My Heart Is Trying to Say?

Are you asleep yet?
Are you awake?
Can you hear what my heart is trying to say?
I call your name softly
I have so much to say

I wanna tell you that I missed you today
Tonight as every other night I wanna share with you what I
really feel like deep inside

This fire that burns like wood covered with ice and no need
for an initial spark
It burns like no other fire I've ever known

Yellow, blue, violet, purple, and red too

Yellow for the friendship you and I built from a common
struggle that did us wrong

Blue for the world I once knew
Violet for the confusion that threatens you
Purple for the choice I made for us to be
And red for the love I never knew

Are you asleep yet?
Are you awake?
Can you hear what my heart is trying to say?

I'm afraid to speak
You might think I'm a fool with nothing better to say
I'm afraid you don't feel the same
You might not even think of us as I do
I'm afraid you'll never tell me you love me
I'm afraid to let you know I do

Epilogue

Our existence as human beings is mainly defined by emotions that impotently surface at any given time. Whether or not these emotions are negative or positive is completely irrelevant. What really matters is listening to your heart, spirit, and mind to find the answers to any question our souls might have. Furthermore, we humans are defined by self-discovery that can only be found deep within our hearts.

Breaking Down the Wall of Silence is a book designed to illuminate and expose the reader to the concept of self-discovery within Jesus Christ. That said, I would like to thank you, the reader, for completing reading *BDWS* and allowing the writings to touch your heart. In the words of William Arthur Ward, "Remember the wonderful blessings that come to you each day from the hands of a generous and gracious God, and forget the irritations that would detract from your happiness."

Baby Carlos

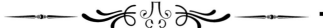

About the Author
1981 – 2007

Carlos Alberto Rivera

It is often said that God wants the best surrounding him in heaven; this truly explains why Carlos Alberto Rivera is at God's side today.

Born on August 30, 1981, in San Salvador, El Salvador, Carlos enter the world during a turbulent period in Central America's history. He started life facing difficult challenges, but together with his family, he went on to overcome these challenges to lead a life that had a positive impact on so many people throughout the Americas–from Montevideo to Manitoba.

Carlos matured at a very early age as he assisted his parents Maria Elena and Carlos with their three young sons Javier, Hugo, and Alvaro. He worked tirelessly and selflessly to ensure that his brothers were well cared for throughout their lives as it took them from El Salvador to Guatemala, Uruguay, and Canada. Carlos served as a guiding influence in their lives and always encouraged them to strive for better things.

Carlos was an exceptionally gifted artist and poet. He expressed his creativity through sketches, paintings, animation, architectural drawings, and poems. He pursued a degree in architecture which he saw as an outlet for his creativity.

Carlos was truly one of those exceptional people that we meet so rarely in our lives. He was a giant to all those who were so fortunate to have met him. His life is a beautiful story and an example to all of us that despite the challenges you face in life, you should always strive to become a better person and to improve your condition and those around you.

This book is dedicated to the creative and artistic spirit of Carlos Rivera and to keeping his beautiful gift alive in all of us.

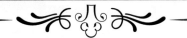

Hugo Rivera on Carlos

In January 1996, my family arrived in Manitoba, Canada. My brother Carlos, at the age of thirteen, started eighth grade without knowing any English. He was the brightest of the four brothers and learned the language fairly quickly. When he started high school, he took on a part-time job at mcdonalds and was still able to be a great student. He always thought of helping the family financially, even when he was just a young boy back in our native country. Carlos had many talents; the ones that stood out the most were his artistic skills and poetry. As far as I can remember, he was the best or one of the best in the school. Every year he had his artwork posted in the school yearbook. His skills continued to develop dramatically. We moved from Manitoba to Ontario, Canada, where he began twelfth grade, and again he was one of the best artists in his school. People were always asking him to draw pictures, including portraits and landscapes out of any medium. He drew many and gave them away. He graduated and moved on to the University of Windsor to study business administration. Carlos finished his first year and decided that business administration was not for him. He moved to Florida, and lived with our mom for about a year. He worked, but mainly he just wanted to spend some time with our mother since she lives so far away. He moved back to Ontario, and as the eldest, he brought his three brothers and we lived in his apartment like a family. It was great living together, even though at times we had our moments and arguments. Carlos was a great cook and always made something out of a recipe book; one thing he cooked often was spaghetti. During the holidays, he would prepare a nice dinner for us all, and I can still remember how delicious it was. Carlos was the head and heart of the family in those days–taking care of me and my other two brothers–because at the time, it was difficult to get a job and our youngest brother was in school. It was quite a responsibility but he managed with few complaints.

Alvaro Rivera on Carlos

Carlos was such a good person and brother because he cared so much about us that he didn't even have time for himself. He would always put family first and himself second. His goal was to make us better in any way possible and that had to do with him being the eldest brother. I can recall many times when he would always help me out with my homework or even with financial problems. Being the youngest, he would always take care of me the most because he felt like he was a dad to me, and I felt that way too. After I moved in with my other brother, Javier, the one thing that my Carlos loved was visiting us. But what he loved the most was spending time with his little nephew Ricardo. Carlos loved him so much as

if he was his own son. He took him everywhere–to the park, to the mall, to eat–he took him all over the place. Sometimes I used to think he was Superman because of all the things he did. He managed many things: he had two jobs, and he also went to college and had time to visit us on the regular basis. He did it all. To me, Carlos was the best of the brothers because he was the person that I could count on the most. He was there for me at all times and never said no. When I was stranded, I would always call him to pick me up and without hesitation, he would say, "Yes, I will be there soon." During our childhood and after moving to Canada where we all searched for a better life, Carlos was the most successful in finding it. He accomplished things quickly and he always wanted perfection in anything that he did. One of the things Carlos did the best was giving good advice, especially to me. He would let me know when I was doing a good thing and when I was doing the wrong thing. Carlos touched many peoples' lives. He had a major impact even on those who barely knew him. Carlos will always be a champion in my eyes and in everyone's eyes. He will never be forgotten.

Javier Rivera on Carlos

There is one thing I remember the most, and that's when he got his first job back in El Salvador, he was only eight. I remember that he would give the money to my mom, he was always thinking for the well being of all of us. He was always helping all of us do our home work, I knew that I was bless to have a brother that cared and that would make time for all of us. His friends meant a lot to him, he would make friends any where he would go, and he has so many friends in El Salvador, Guatemala, Uruguay Miami and Canada. When it would rain or snow a lot, and he new that I got out work he would call my house to see if I got home ok. I started doing the same, calling him to check if he got home ok. He also would ask me time to time if I had food or if I was ok with money. Some times he would bring us food, wow he was a great cook, I love his soups. That's the kind of brother that he was, always making sure we where alright. He loved my son so much, every time he would come to the house, he would bring him a toy. He would take my son out to eat or he would take him for walks', he loved spending time with my son. I spend more time with him when my car broke down, he would give me a ride anytime anywhere, and for two weeks he took me to work, at that time he was working nights and he would get up at six am just so he could give me a ride, sometimes he would let me use the car and he would take the bus to his second job at the mall, he would never complain, he will always be my hero I wish everybody would have a heart like my brothers, and for sure this planet would be a better place.

Maria Elena Balcazar on son Carlos

I Maria Elena Balcazar as a mother of Carlos Rivera, first of all I want to thank God for giving me a great son, caring, cheerful, loving who always was willing to help others without hesitation and always there for his brothers.

He was more than my son, he was my best friend, my protector someone who I could always count on.

When my son was born he filled my heart with joy, he was my everything and now that he is gone, he left my heart empty. I missed him so much, I need him like the air to breathe.

Now that he is gone I feel his presence close to me like he is looking over me, I will always love him and have him in my heart until the last day of my life.

I would like to thank on his behalf to all the rest of the family members and to all the people that made my son's dream come true.

Thank you so much especially to Sarai Diaz, Stefano Pontoni and Janice Quieta for allowinsg us to use some of her photographs of Carlos.

Carlos in Cuba

Carlos with brother - Carlos leaning against the tree, Hugo, Javier and Alvaro

Carlos with brothers

Carlos with parents for his High School Graduation- Maria Elena Balcazar, Carlos & Carlos Rivera

Printed in the United States
by Baker & Taylor Publisher Services